*Other* WALL STREET JOURNAL. *books*

THE WALL STREET JOURNAL. *Portfolio of Business Cartoons*

THE WALL STREET JOURNAL. *Portfolio of Women in Business*

*Available from* **DOW JONES** *at*
**(800) 635-8349**

# THE WALL STREET JOURNAL.

## Portfolio of

## cartoons.com

# THE WALL STREET JOURNAL.

*Portfolio of*

*cartoons.com*

**Edited by CHARLES PRESTON**

*Published by*

# THE WALL STREET JOURNAL.

ISBN 1-881944-29-8

Books can be purchased in bulk at special discounts.
For information please call (800) 635-8349, Dow Jones & Company.

The Wall Street Journal
200 Liberty Street
New York, NY 10281

Printed in the United States of America
1 2 3 4 5 6 7 8
First Edition

# THE WALL STREET JOURNAL.

## Portfolio of

## cartoons.com

"I don't care what it is–if it's got
'dot com' in the title, buy it."

"*Actually, the computers are up but I'm down.*"

*"And be sure to check out my Happiness Web site!"*

"*As fate would have it, our computers are down. You'll have to wait in limbo a while longer, Mr. Potts.*"

"*As I understand it, it emits a sound only they can hear.*"

"*You can't report him to the CEO.*
*He is the CEO.*"

"*Can you take time out from your e-mail and your voice mail to read your mail mail?*"

"Combination #3 is also available in
an upgraded #3.3 version."

"No, *this* is the afterlife.
Cyberspace is over there."

"Before computers and word processors,
we were nerds with slide rules and
very sharp pencils."

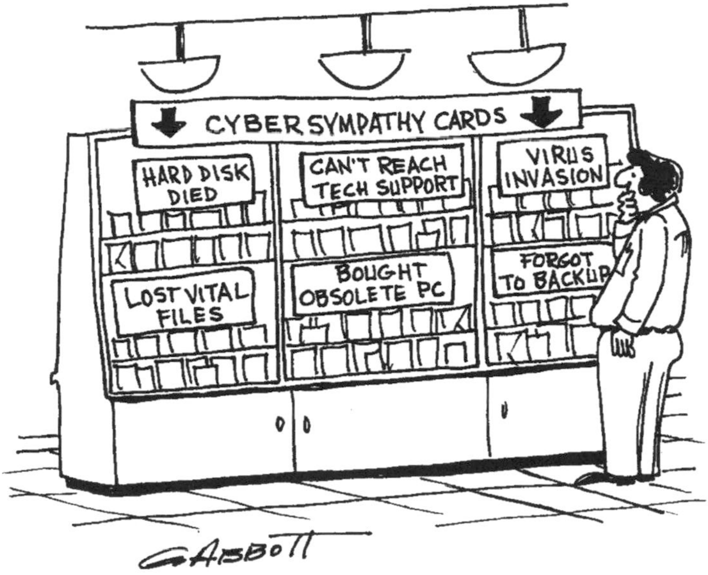
CYBER SYMPATHY CARDS
HARD DISK DIED
CAN'T REACH TECH SUPPORT
VIRUS INVASION
LOST VITAL FILES
BOUGHT OBSOLETE PC
FORGOT TO BACKUP
GABBOTT

"He ate my computer mouse."

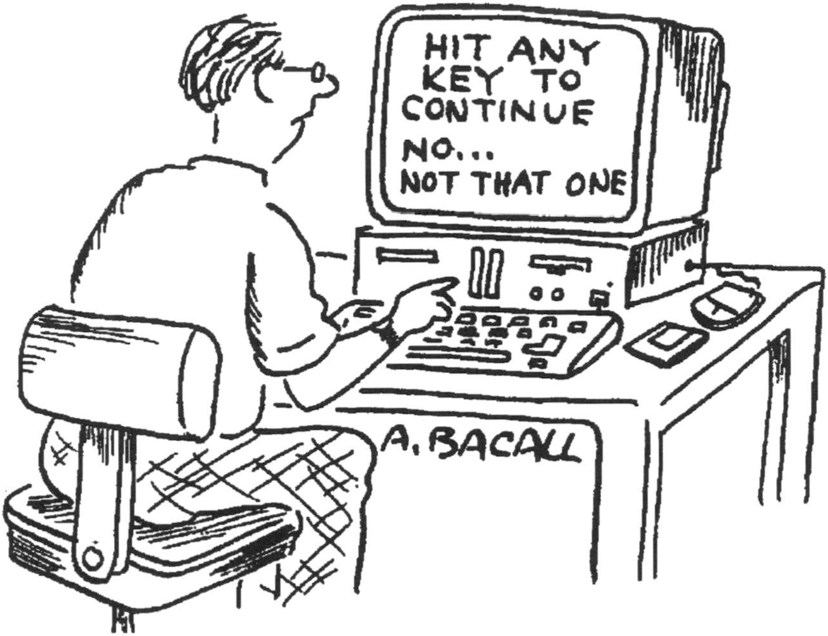
HIT ANY KEY TO CONTINUE
NO...
NOT THAT ONE
A. BACALL

"*Now, **tell Daddy** exactly *what*
*you double-clicked on.*"

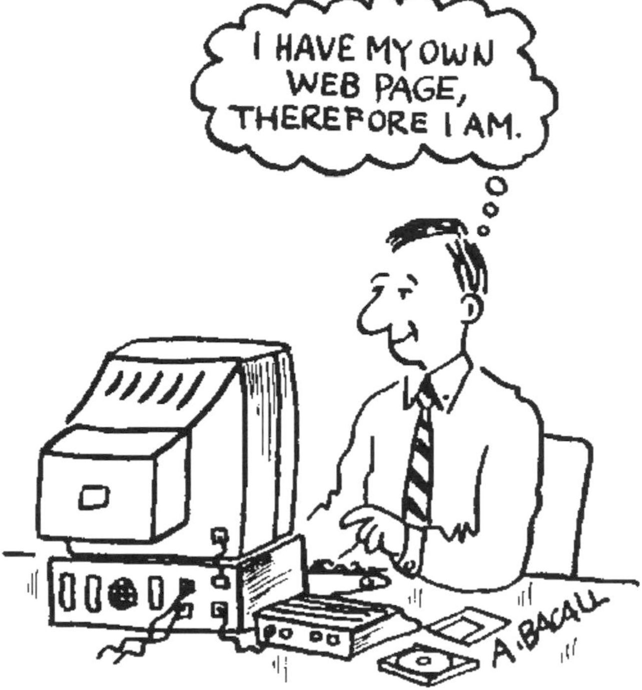
I HAVE MY OWN WEB PAGE, THEREFORE I AM.
A. BACALL

*"I must admit, I prefer the old traditional method of signaling to the pitcher."*

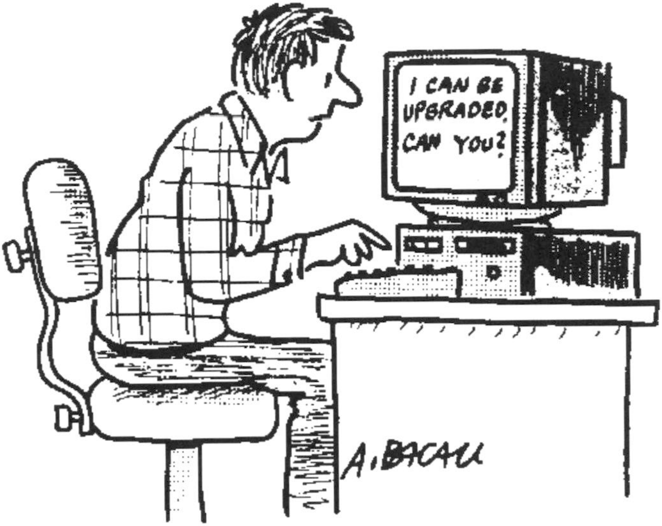
I CAN BE UPGRADED. CAN YOU?
A. BACALL

"*He followed me home from his Web site!
Can I keep him? Please???*"

*"It wants to go to Silicon Valley to discover its roots!"*

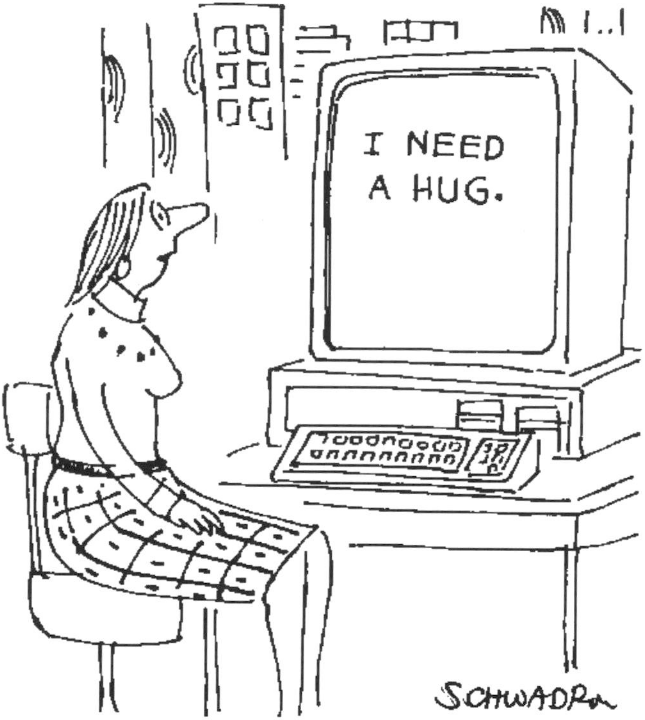
I NEED
A HUG.
SCHWADRON

"I telecommute from home, but twice
a day I log onto goofoff.com and hang
out at the virtual water cooler."

"*Thanks. It's been fun bouncing microwaves off your skull, too.*"

"*I was going to fax it to you, but that seemed too impersonal, so I'm going to e-mail it to you.*"

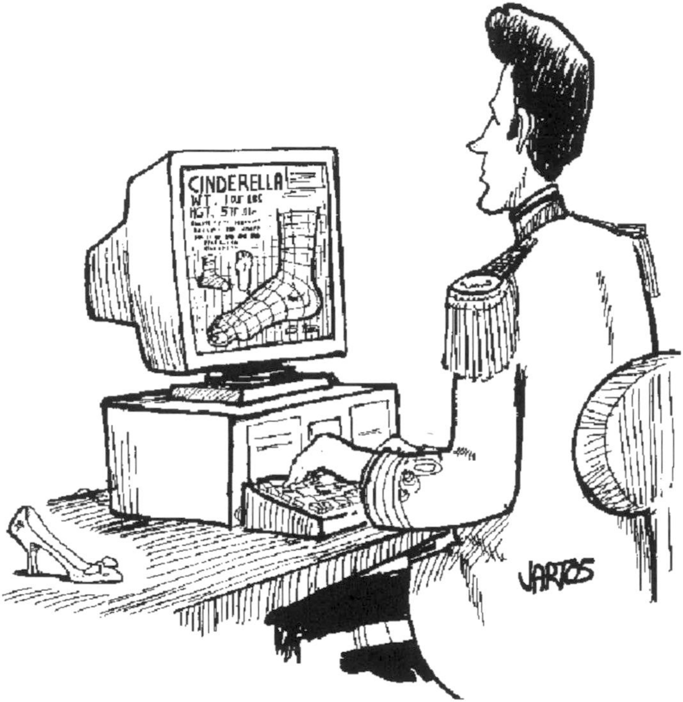
CINDERELLA

*"I'll try, but I've never debugged*
*a program before."*

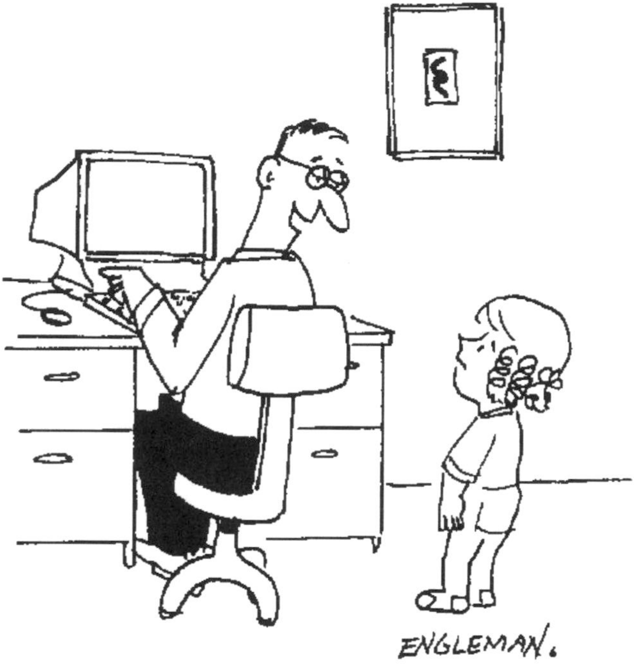
ENGLEMAN.

*"Go back to your room . . . turn on your computer, and Daddy will e-mail you a bedtime story."*

"*It's imperative that I talk to someone* now."

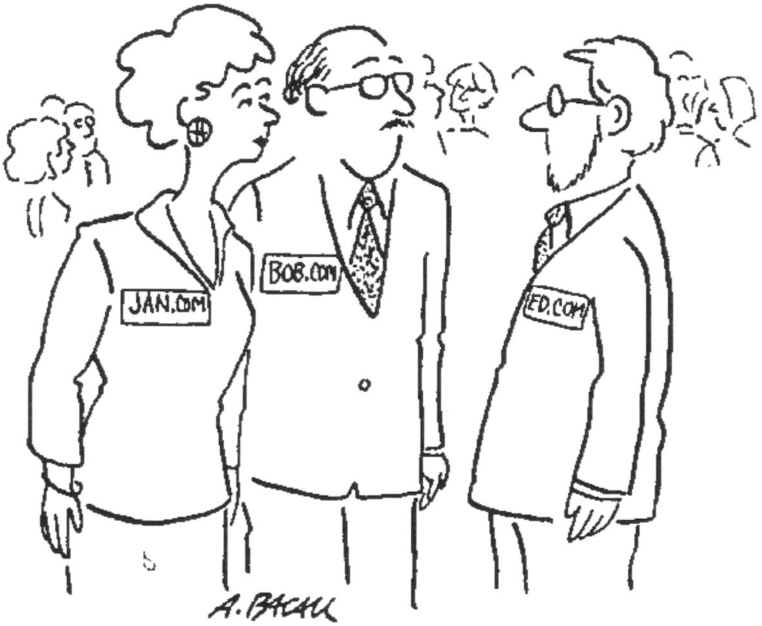
JAN.COM
BOB.COM
ED.COM
A. BACALL

"*Oh, the commute to work was a breeze,
but I've been stuck in Internet
traffic for four hours!*"

"If you don't find what you want on
our 'specials' board, you may return
to the main menu for other options."

"I told you 'bomb.com' was a
lousy name for a Web site."

"*Oh, I have loads of experience.*
*Would you like to see a CD-ROM of me working?*"

"*Let's go for a walk . . . your micro-cap
stocks will still be there when you get back.*"

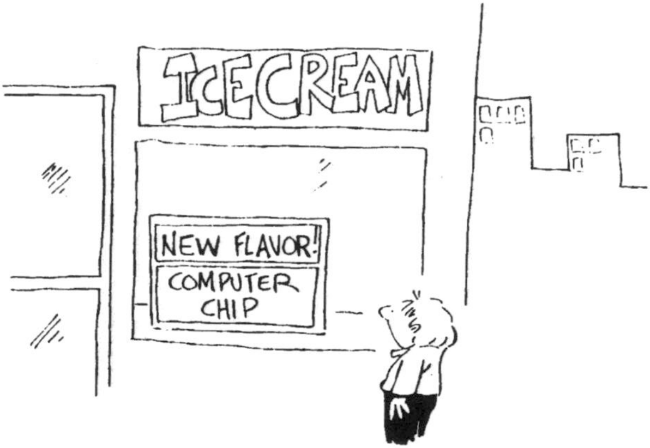
ICECREAM
NEW FLAVOR!
COMPUTER CHIP

"*I don't care how much he knows about computers—if he calls me 'Dude' one more time he's out of here.*"

"Santa.com just isn't the same
as getting those letters."

"I'm sorry, he's not available at the
moment—both Mr. Dobbs and his
computer have just frozen."

"I'm sorry. One of our Internet customers
just outbid you for your 8 o'clock table."

"*I think you'll find I've crossed all the T's and dotted all the coms.*"

"I'm glad I made mine before this
high tech stuff took over."

"*I'm not good with names, but I never forget a Web site.*"

*"Is your computer virus ready for
our pot yet, Mildred?"*

"*Miss Spencer, I want you to e-mail this memo to every man, woman and child on the face of the earth.*"

*"I'm sorry, but you're only allowed entry under your main screen name."*

"Ms. Collins, have someone bring me
my password."

"Nobody in there knows. I don't know.
You don't know. Just what do you suppose
a 'price-to-earnings ratio' means?"

*"Really? I wasn't aware we had a cyberpunk division."*

"She buys all her supplies online.
She does all her schmoozing in chat rooms and
downloads all her jokes from the Web. So you see,
she has no need to deal through a salesman."

*"So you visit www.birds+bees.com, OK?"*

"Sorry to drag you all the way out here,
but actually I was looking for tech support."

"Fired? There must be some mistake—I just
joined a chat group of upwardly mobile
young professionals!"

"*Stephen, you can't telecommute to* church."

*"Summer vacation has officially started.
I dumped my memory bank on the way home!"*

"The only way I could gain access
to my hospital records was to tap
into their computer."

"*Who changed the password to 'Arf'?*"

"*This is Ed. He's the nerve center of our entire operation.*"

"*We bust out tonight at midnight . . . according to the Internet.*"

"We don't need to ask questions;
everything we need to know is
on the computer."

"*We've decided to offer full partnership to your computer instead.*"

*"What's all this talk I hear about
a World Wide Web?"*

"*Well, I'm going to double-click on the tuna sandwich.*"

"Why don't you concentrate on the
Great American Software instead?"

"*With this computer, I'm interconnected
with all other gurus, so I can give you
a more reliable version of the truth.*"

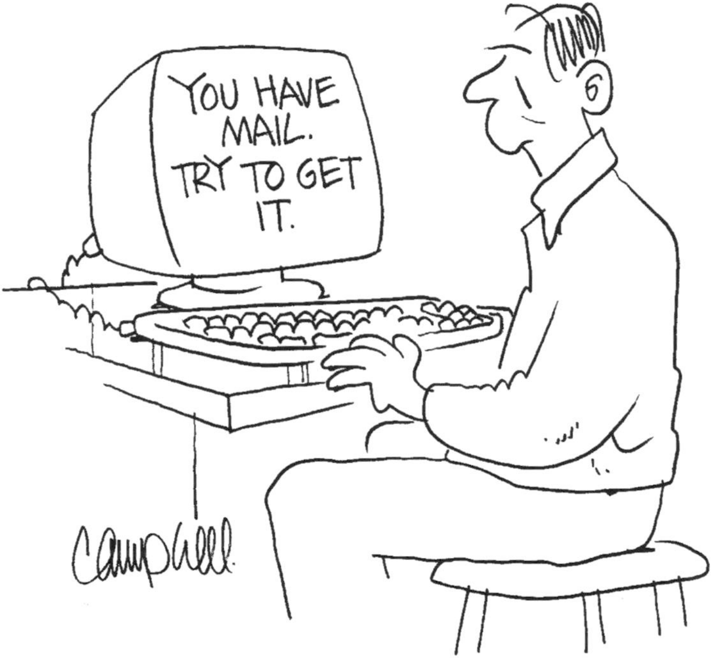
YOU HAVE MAIL. TRY TO GET IT.
Campbell

"*Wow, I wasn't even aware that the old boys' network had a Web site!*"

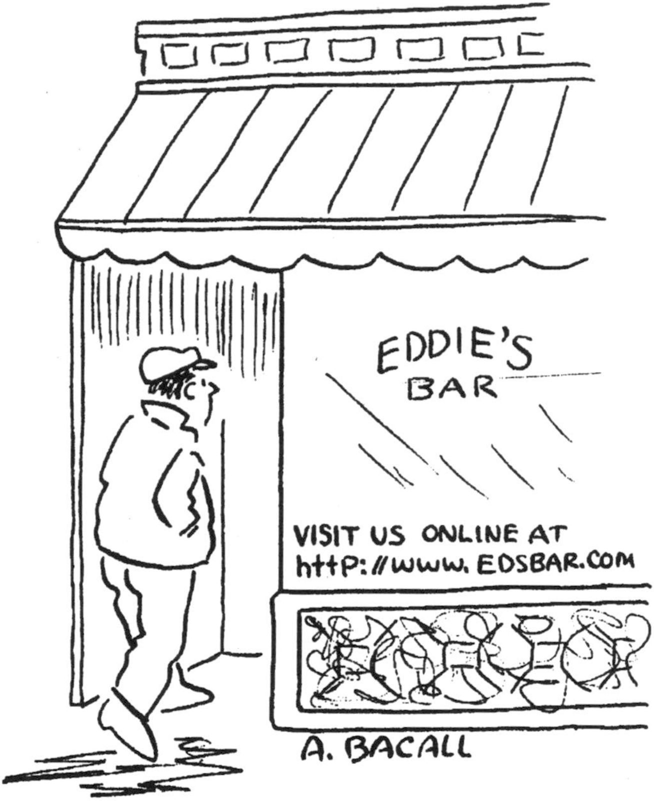
EDDIE'S
BAR
VISIT US ONLINE AT
http://www.EDSBAR.COM
A. BACALL

*"Excuse me, but is this office space taken?"*

"*And if you ever want more advice,
Daniel, my e-mail address is
grandpa@x.com.*"

"*Write a letter to Santa? It's easier just to break into his computer distribution system.*"

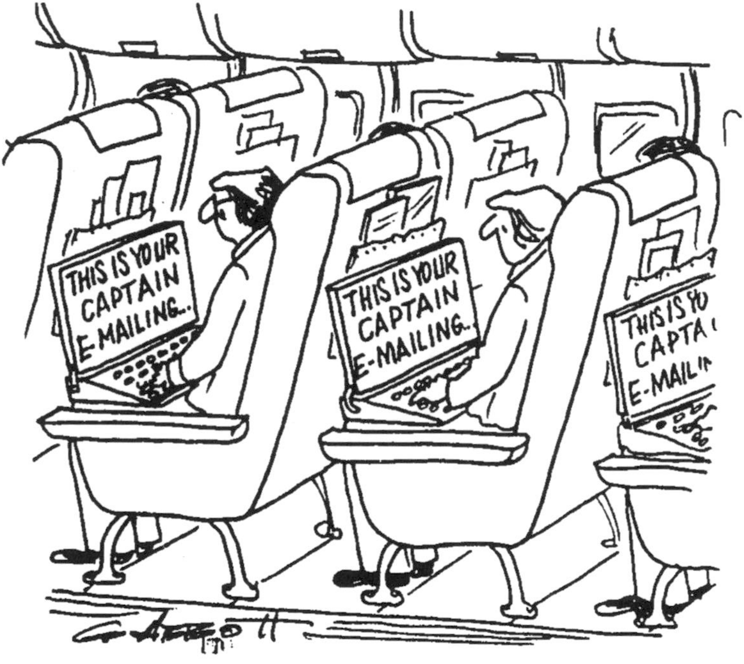
THIS IS YOUR CAPTAIN E-MAILING...
THIS IS YOUR CAPTAIN E-MAILING...

"*He always barks whenever the electronic mail arrives!*"

"*Well, I know how to be at one with nature, and* still *have my phone with me.*"

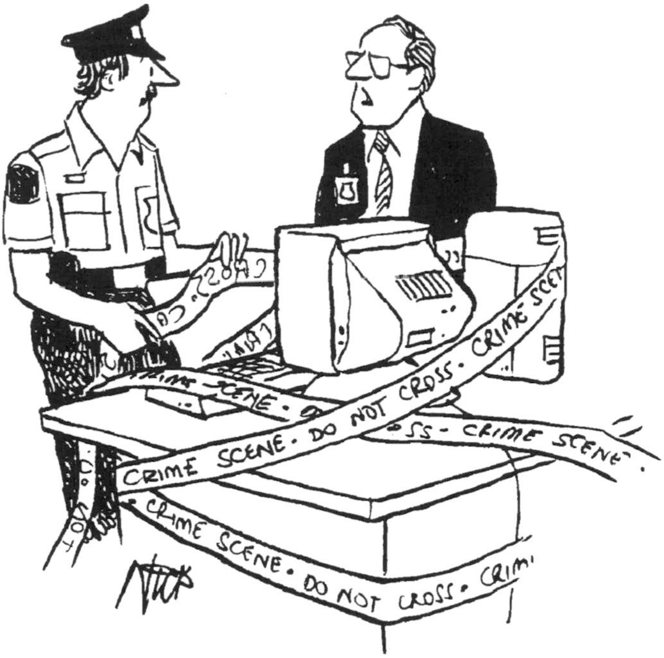
CRIME SCENE • DO NOT CROSS • CRIME SCENE
SS • CRIME SCENE
CRIME SCENE • DO NOT CROSS • CRIM

*"White-collar crime?"*

"We've got his e-mail, fax, pager, cell phone, voice mail and private line but absolutely no reason to contact him."

*"Yeah, I'm not allowed to cross the street,
but with the Internet, who cares?"*

"I'll admit I haven't been a very good
Internet provider."

"*Exactly when was 'Have a nice day' replaced
with 'Please visit our Web site'?*"

"*Careful, sir–they can sense fear.*"

"Today we're featuring Grilled Cyberfish,
a succulent variety caught on the Net."

*"Thank you for calling Cyberbiz.com.
How may I direct your call?"*

*"All this, and without a cash flow."*

*"What rhymes with dot.com?"*

"Funny, I never would have guessed you were a .com. You look like a .org or a .edu."

"Now *you* *tell me* you have a Web site!"

# *Index of Cartoonists*

Charles Preston edits the "Pepper . . . and Salt" cartoon feature, which appears daily on the editorial pages of The Wall Street Journal and WSJ.com. To subscribe, call 1-800-JOURNAL or go to http://services.wsj.com.